977.1
LEE

14730

Leebrick, Kristal

The lucky buckeye

DATE DUE			

North Shore Community School
Library
5926 Ryan Road
Duluth, MN 55804

THE LUCKY BUCKEYE

~ A Story About Ohio ~

Written by Kristal Leebrick

Illustrated by Bob Doucet

Consulting Editor, Diane Craig, M.A./Reading Specialist

ABDO
Publishing Company

Published by ABDO Publishing Company
8000 West 78th Street, Edina, Minnesota 55439.

Printed in the United States.

Editor: Pam Price
Content Developer: Nancy Tuminelly
Cover and Interior Design and Production:
    Anders Hanson, Mighty Media
Photo Credits: Ed Conners, Corbis Images, iStockphoto
(Terry J. Alcorn, Andrew Hill), One Mile Up, Shutterstock,
Quarter-dollar coin image from the United States Mint.

Library of Congress Cataloging-in-Publication Data

Leebrick, Kristal, 1958-
  The lucky buckeye : a story about Ohio / Kristal Leebrick ;
Illustrated by Bob Doucet.
    p. cm. -- (Fact & fable. State stories)
  ISBN 978-1-60453-185-5
  1. Ohio--Juvenile literature. I. Doucet, Bob, ill. II. Title.

  F491.3.L44 2009
  977.1--dc22

                            2008019358

Super SandCastle™ books are created by a team of
professional educators, reading specialists, and content
developers around five essential components—phonemic
awareness, phonics, vocabulary, text comprehension,
and fluency—to assist young readers as they develop
reading skills and strategies and increase their general
knowledge. All books are written, reviewed, and leveled
for guided reading, early reading intervention, and
Accelerated Reader® programs for use in shared, guided,
and independent reading and writing activities to
support a balanced approach to literacy instruction.

TABLE OF CONTENTS

cardinal
(pg. 9)

Toledo

Sandusky
(pg. 10)

Cuyahoga
River
(pg. 5)

Akron

Lima

OHIO

Columbus Zoo
(pg. 16)

Steubenville

buckeye
(pg. 15)

Columbus

Dayton

Marietta

Cincinnati

Serpent Mound
(pg. 13)

Wayne National
Forest (pg. 7)

Ohio River

LEGEND

☆ CAPITAL   ● STORY START

○ CITY   - - - STORY PATH

〰 RIVER   ✳ STORY END

White-Tailed Deer

The white-tailed deer is Ohio's official state mammal. The deer almost disappeared from Ohio one hundred years ago when people were allowed to hunt all year. Now deer can be hunted only at certain times of the year.

THE LUCKY BUCKEYE

Grandfather Deer was the oldest and wisest white-tailed deer in Ohio. Bucky loved to hear Grandfather's stories about Ohio. His favorite was about the day the Cuyahoga River caught fire near Cleveland. "It was probably a spark from a passing train that started the fire," Grandfather would say. "All the creatures that lived around the river knew it would happen one day."

The dark and dirty Cuyahoga River was full of oil and waste from factories. It was also polluted with trash and jammed with logs. "People treated that river like a trash can! The fire finally forced people to treat the river with respect," said Grandfather.

Cuyahoga River

Cuyahoga means "crooked river" in the Iroquois language. The hundred-mile-long Cuyahoga River flows into Lake Erie. The river caught fire 10 times between 1868 and 1969.

Ohio River

Ohio is a Native American word that means "great river." The Ohio River is one of the longest rivers in North America. It is the southern border of Ohio.

Grandfather Deer and Bucky lived in the forest near the Ohio River. That's a long way from Cleveland, but Bucky had heard the Cuyahoga River story his whole life. Grandfather was one of the state's most famous storytellers. He traveled to festivals all over Ohio to share his tales.

Grandfather was getting ready to go to a festival in Cleveland. He wanted to take Bucky along. Bucky didn't want to go. He had never been away from his home in the forest. But Grandfather was so excited about them traveling together that Bucky agreed to go. He wanted to please Grandfather, but he was still worried about leaving home.

Wayne National Forest

Wayne National Forest is the only national forest in Ohio. People go there to hike, camp, canoe, and fish.

Southern Ohio Storytelling Festival

The Southern Ohio Storytelling Festival is held in Chillicothe, Ohio. For two days, storytellers from around the country tell tales that are sometimes true and sometimes made up.

As they started on their journey, Grandfather said, "Bucky, today reminds me of the day I went with Great Grandfather to my first festival in Chillicothe. I'll tell you a little story." Bucky said nothing. He wasn't listening. Bucky just dragged his hooves on the ground and thought about home.

Bucky didn't want to tell Grandfather that he was afraid. His forest friends told many stories about Ohio that made him very fearful. His friend Carl, a red cardinal, especially liked telling scary tales to all the young creatures who lived in the forest.

Cardinal

The cardinal is the state bird of Ohio. Male cardinals are bright red and female cardinals are reddish brown. Their dull coloring helps females hide while they are nesting.

9

Cedar Point Amusement Park

Cedar Point is located in Sandusky, Ohio. It is called the roller coaster capital of the world. There are 17 roller coasters in the park!

Just the other day, Carl told Bucky about a strange park near Lake Erie. "It is a place where humans fly faster than birds down giant metal mountains called roller coasters!" Carl said. He'd heard that some people went so fast that their mouths froze open! This scared Bucky. He didn't want to see or ride those scary things.

The local ladybugs also had stories to tell. Bucky overheard them chattering about a snake hill just north of the forest. He was really frightened of snakes. Bucky tried his hardest not to think about his fears. He wished there was something that would help him not be so afraid about being away from home.

Ladybug

The Ohio state insect is the ladybug. But it isn't really a bug. It's a ladybird beetle! The ladybug is said to be proud and friendly, just like the people of Ohio.

Black Racer Snake

The Ohio state reptile is the black racer snake. Farmers like the snake because it eats mice and other animals that harm their crops. The black racer bites when it's scared, but it is not poisonous.

Bucky and Grandfather walked toward a grassy hill. "Hey, kid, watch it!" said a voice.

Bucky looked down and saw a black racer snake! "Yikes!" he yelled.

Grandfather saw the snake and chuckled. "Shadow, my friend, how are you?" said Grandfather.

"Grandfather Deer, nice to see you again," the snake hissed.

"Shadow, meet my grandson, Bucky," Grandfather replied.

"Pleased to meet you," Shadow said as she slithered closer to them.

Bucky was shaking. "Shadow is an old friend of mine. She's the Serpent Mound's caretaker. For someone so low to the ground, she sure can tell one tall tale," Grandfather joked.

"S-s-serpent Mound," Bucky stuttered. "Isn't that the snake hill?"

Serpent Mound

Serpent Mound was built by ancient Native Americans. They built it in the shape of a huge snake. Scientists are still trying to learn more about when and why it was built.

13

"Actually," Shadow said, "Serpent Mound is not covered with snakes. It's just shaped like a snake." Then Shadow said, "Hey, I'm yearning to tell a yarn or two. May I join you?" The two deer agreed. Shadow slid along beside them. They passed fields of tomato plants and came to some flowering trees.

Tomato Juice

Until about 200 years ago, people thought tomatoes were poisonous. Today tomato juice is the Ohio state beverage. Only California makes more tomato juice than Ohio.

14

"Those are buckeye trees. A buckeye seed looks like a buck's eye," Shadow explained.

"Some say that buckeye seeds bring good luck," said Grandfather.

Bucky grabbed a seed and tied it around his neck. "Maybe this will make me feel less scared," he thought.

Buckeye

The buckeye is the Ohio state tree. Ohio State University's football team is called the Ohio State Buckeyes. Ohio's nickname is the Buckeye State.

Columbus

Columbus is the Ohio state capital. The city was named for Christopher Columbus. The Columbus Zoo and Aquarium is known around the world for its animal collections.

Soon the three travelers arrived in Columbus. They spent the night at the zoo. They snacked on buckeye candy from the food stands and swapped stories with the penguins, kangaroos, and tigers. Early the next day, Grandfather, Bucky, and Shadow continued on their adventure. Bucky looked down at his buckeye and realized he felt no fear.

Buckeye Candy

1 stick softened butter
1¾ cups creamy peanut butter
1 teaspoon vanilla
1 pound powdered sugar
1 12-ounce package semisweet chocolate chips

Cream together the butter, peanut butter, and vanilla. Add the powdered sugar and beat until the mixture is smooth. Roll the candy into one-inch balls and place them on waxed paper. Melt the chocolate chips in a double boiler. Dip each ball into the chocolate, covering most of the candy. Place the candy on wax paper to cool. Makes 8 dozen.

When they got to Sandusky, they could hear loud rumbling and people screaming. A horse pulling a buggy full of people went by. The horse grumbled, "I'm glad my people don't go there."

"Where?" Bucky asked.

"The roller coaster park!" shouted Shadow. "Let's go!"

Bucky looked at his buckeye again. Then he leaped on the Switchback Railway and had the time of his life! Bucky begged to ride again and again, but it was time to leave.

Amish

Ohio has the largest population of Amish people in the world. Most Amish don't believe in owning modern inventions such as cell phones, televisions, computers, and cars.

Clean Water Act of 1972

The Clean Water Act made it illegal for cities and factories to dump waste into the country's rivers, lakes, streams, and wetlands. The act was originally called the Federal Water Pollution Control Act.

Finally they reached the Cuyahoga River near Cleveland. Bucky was a little nervous that the river would catch fire again. "There's no need to be scared," said Grandfather. "The water is much cleaner now, and people are more careful about taking care of the river." Bucky looked at his buckeye and felt relieved.

Later, at the festival, Grandfather told about Johnny Appleseed planting apple trees throughout Ohio. Then Shadow told about the red carnation becoming the state flower. Then it was Bucky's turn. He looked at his buckeye and began, "Once there was a young deer who was afraid to leave home. But his wise grandfather took him on a grand adventure." Grandfather Deer and Shadow listened with delight!

THE END

Johnny Appleseed

Johnny Appleseed was a folk hero whose real name was John Chapman. He helped pioneers plant apple trees throughout Ohio and the Midwest.

OHIO AT A GLANCE

Abbreviation:
OH

Capital:
Columbus

Largest city: Columbus
(15th-largest U.S. city)

Statehood: March 1, 1803
(17th state)

Area:
44,828 sq. mi.
(116,104 sq km)
(34th-largest state)

Nickname:
Buckeye State

Motto:
With God all things
are possible

State bird: cardinal

State flower:
red carnation

State tree: buckeye

State mammal:
white-tailed deer

State insect: ladybug

State song:
"Beautiful Ohio"

STATE SEAL

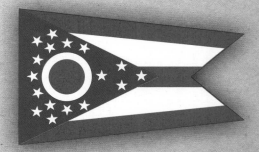

STATE FLAG

The Ohio quarter features an astronaut and an early aircraft. It honors the state's contribution to the history of aviation. Pioneers of aviation Neil Armstrong, John Glenn, and Orville Wright were all born in Ohio.

STATE QUARTER

What Do You Know?

How well do you remember the story? Match the pictures to the questions below! Then check your answers at the bottom of the page!

 **a.** black racer snake

 **b.** buckeye seed

 **c.** cardinal

 **d.** roller coaster

 **e.** Cuyahoga River

 **f.** snake hill

1. Which river caught fire?

2. What kind of animal is Bucky's friend Carl?

3. What did Bucky hear the ladybugs talking about?

4. What kind of creature is Shadow?

5. What did Bucky tie around his neck?

6. What kind of ride is the Switchback Railway?

What to Do in Ohio

1 Tour a candy factory

Spangler Store & Museum, Bryan

2 See hippos underwater

Hippoquarium at the Toledo Zoo, Toledo

3 Celebrate rock and roll

Rock and Roll Hall of Fame and Museum, Cleveland

4 Attend a popcorn festival

Marion Popcorn Festival, Marion

5 Visit an alpaca farm

Alpaca Spring Valley Farm, Minerva

6 Watch fireworks

Red, White and Boom! Columbus

7 Explore nature

Hocking Hills State Park, Logan

8 Learn about slavery

National Underground Railroad Freedom Center, Cincinnati

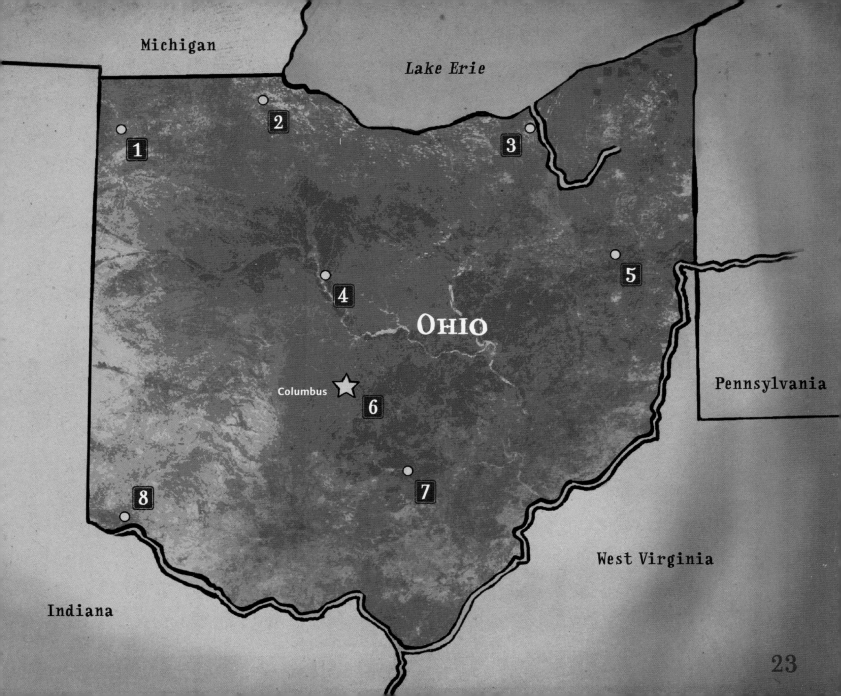

Michigan

Lake Erie

1

2

3

OHIO

4

5

Columbus

6

7

8

Indiana

West Virginia

Pennsylvania

23

GLOSSARY

beverage – a liquid that you drink, such as milk, juice, or soda.

buggy – a cart for people to ride in that is pulled by one horse.

chuckle – to laugh quietly.

crooked – having bends and curves.

festival – a celebration that happens at the same time each year.

grumble – to complain in a low voice.

mammal – a warm-blooded animal that has hair and whose females produce milk to feed the young.

pioneer – 1) one of the first people to settle in an area. 2) someone who helps create a new method or a new way of thinking.

serpent – a snake.

wetland – a low, wet area of land such as a swamp or a marsh.

yearn – to want very much.

About SUPER SANDCASTLE™

Bigger Books for Emerging Readers
Grades K–4

Created for library, classroom, and at-home use, Super SandCastle™ books support and engage young readers as they develop and build literacy skills and will increase their general knowledge about the world around them. Super SandCastle™ books are part of SandCastle™, the leading PreK–3 imprint for emerging and beginning readers. Super SandCastle™ features a larger trim size for more reading fun.

Let Us Know

Super SandCastle™ would like to hear your stories about reading this book. What was your favorite page? Was there something hard that you needed help with? Share the ups and downs of learning to read. We want to hear from you! Send us an e-mail.

sandcastle@abdopublishing.com

Contact us for a complete list of SandCastle™, Super SandCastle™, and other nonfiction and fiction titles from ABDO Publishing Company.

www.abdopublishing.com • 8000 West 78th Street Edina, MN 55439 • 800-800-1312 • 952-831-1632 fax